A Path to Living Your Dreams:

An Invitation to Power, Peace and Love

by

One Path

authorHOUSE™

1663 LIBERTY DRIVE, SUITE 200
BLOOMINGTON, INDIANA 47403
(800) 839-8640
WWW.AUTHORHOUSE.COM

This book is a work of non-fiction. Unless otherwise noted, the author and the publisher make no explicit guarantees as to the accuracy of the information contained in this book and in some cases, names of people and places have been altered to protect their privacy.

© 2004 One Path. All Rights Reserved.

No part of this book may be reproduced, stored in a retrieval system, or transmitted by any means without the written permission of the author.

First published by AuthorHouse 11/23/04

ISBN: 1-4208-1181-9(sc)

Printed in the United States of America
Bloomington, Indiana

This book is printed on acid-free paper.

Acknowledgments

I could not have written this book without the presence of love, therefore:

Thanks to: My parents, Paul & Elizabeth Mutiva, who intuitively understand and use their creative power to be generous with others. Mother & Father, thank you for your patience and support. Thank you for believing in me.

Thanks to my younger sister who speaks to me with ageless wisdom. Thank you so much for helping me with this book, Kiki. You are my inspiration.

Thank you, Hanan Abdul-Salaam, for being the second person to read my manuscript and for providing me with positive feedback. You have been a tremendous help and a wonderful friend.

Thank you, Ayodeji Metiko, for choosing to demonstrate and to experience unconditional friendship with me.

Thanks to my Warrior friends: Aho! From, One Path.

Thanks to Luz Brissett, little Aston & Greg Williams. Luz, know that you have been aptly named. You bring light into the world—you bring light into mine.

Thanks to Fatimah Provillon. You have a love of life and talent that the world longs to see. I see tremendous strength in you.

Thanks to friendship: Rafikieli Mutiva, Nicholas Dennehy, Jackie Krienke, Fatimah Provillon, Lauren McCoy, Kenia Montijo, Keisha Peynado, Farrah Clarke, the Dunphy sisters (Megan, Sarah & Jessica), Denita Patel, Shameeli Singh, Lady Berry...

Thank you, Michael Bajakian. To know you is to witness the unfolding of a champion's heart and mind. I know your eyes.... your smile.... your passion...and I find that there is nowhere I am, where you are not.

Thanks to the beautiful children in my life: Elizabeth Ann & Andrew, Alex & Nia, Serati, Naomi & Sasha, Julius & Jasmine, Farrah's little one, & Michael's Ava. You are joy in my life.

Thank you, Jairus Maloba, for reminding me to be courageous.

Thanks to Oprah Winfrey. I enjoy the love that you express in all that you do.

Thanks to music, for transporting me to the most wondrous experiences of love.

Thanks to: those who mentor me on self-awareness and inspire me to write this book. The messages that I share with you in this book have already been expressed with profound in-sight and eloquence by the following people: James Allen Neale Donald Walsch, Gary Zukav, Eckhart Tolle, Dr. Wayne Dyer, Norman Vincent Peale, Claude Bristol, Linda Grabhorn, T. Harv Ekher, Satori Mateu and Lysa Moskowitz-Mateu, Phil Collins...and many others not mentioned here.

Thank you to my readers. I would not be on this path were you not now choosing to be on it, also.

There are those in spirit form that I also thank: my uncle Patrick, Sheya, my grandparents, my spirit guide and all my ancestors who watch over me and guide me on my journey here on earth. Thanks to the enlightened spirit within me for waking me to wisdom.

Table of Contents

Acknowledgments v

Foreword xi

Our Story 1

One Path 4

Power 6

The Possibility 8

Choices 12

Creation 14

Truth 18

Why Wait? 21

Manifestation 24

Unconditional Value 26

Freedom 29

Past 32

Illusion 35

Blindness 37

The Light 40

Space 42

One-Ness 45

Inner Perspective 47

Opportunity 50

Action 53

Emotion 56

Life Energy 60

Love 64

Fear 67

Peace 70

Decide 74

Abundance 77

Perfection 80

Shape Shifting 85

Saying Goodbye 89

Note to the Reader 91

Foreword

First, understand that I write this book not as a psychologist or any type of behavioral expert. I do not intend for you to agree with, or to accept, or to label anything that I write as 'true' or 'right' or 'fact.' The ideas that I express in this book are my own personal interpretation of this world. They spring from personal life experience and a myriad of what I perceive as "messages" of love.

I write this book as a messenger of that part of life that I have known as good. My intention is to share my story and my perceptions, as they have renewed the life that lay dormant in me for many years. I recently heard that we write what we need to read and teach what we need to learn. I write this book in part for purely selfish reasons, as the act of writing it, is for me the highest expression of life—*creation*. In this book I explore the limitless-ness of being human. It is not a coincidence that I am here and now writing this book. I write because I choose to do so. It is not a coincidence that you are here now reading this book. You read because you choose to do so. In choosing we utilize our creative powers. In creating this book, I assume ultimate power. My hope is that this power shall bring about the re-awakening of power within you and many others.

And so, I feel compelled to speak, to write, to express this deep-seated desire of mine to heal not only my-self but also-our human kind. All of my life, for as long as I can remember, there have been these 'whys.' Like why do we feel that we have to everyday do harm to ourselves to exist as a people in this physical form? My quest for answers once led me to believe in hopelessness.

Yet now...

In me there is a power born-of years-of moments spent. Moments that span for all of us-a thousand years, a million years. A cry so deep, it is unfelt. A longing so profound, it hurts. Unheard, unspoken, unwritten. How can we exist and do nothing? The sadness I had felt for so long, bespeaks how numb we have become, that we should everyday ignore, destroy and implant in our-selves, hearts unfeeling, eyes unseeing, words that seek to disguise, actions that seek to belie, a Greatness denied?

We have snipers, rapists, child molesters, murderers, terrorists-all of whom reflect our world's unconscious pain. I want to make it clear to all who read these words that our world's pain *can* be transformed and that to do nothing about our own pain, is to create more of it in our world. So, join me in this journey towards transformation.

Our Story

I understand that you may be reading this book to find answers to your own life's questions, but I am telling you now that this book has no answers.

I am not writing this book to give you answers to your innermost questions. This I cannot do, because it is something only you can do for yourself.

You have the power to re-write your story of life. You have the power to be however you wish to be, to do whatever you wish to do and to have whatever you wish to have. You have the power to live the life of your dreams.

Within this book is a story. It is the story that I once lived. I share my story to reveal yours. You see, my story is no different from yours. It is the age-old story of our being. And so, it really is *your* story. As it is examined by you and I together, it becomes *our story*. All individual stories become one story. They become the one story that tells the story of life.

One Path

When we are able to share our stories in love, we are reminded of this story. And as we remember this story, we become aware of our power to change it and to live the life of our dreams. So, let us begin remembering now...

Someone took advantage of me in his search for power. In trusting him and because I believed power as external, I became what seemed to me for years, a "victim in life." It seemed as if he had won, and taken something very precious from me-my power...my power to be without fear.

I could not speak or trust openly. When I spoke my voice would tremble, even as I bade it not to. I withdrew from people, stayed in the background, and avoided doing things that might expose my weakness. I had become afraid of life. I watched other people doing things I would not allow myself to do and became very, very... sad. The sadness meshed in with my weakened spirit and swallowed me up. And even as I looked unto beautiful things—flowers blooming, people laughing-no matter what I saw, I felt mainly sadness...

Then, I began to wonder about myself, not quite sure of what to make of how I had become who I had become. The pain in me was tremendous. I knew not how to escape it. I wanted...I wanted...I wanted...and all the things I wanted, were things I felt I could not have.

My life started to change when I made the choice to transform my world. I made the decision to change the way in which I perceive myself and the world around me. Having made that choice, I stepped onto my path.

Go confidently in the direction of your dreams. Live the life you have imagined.

—-Henry David Thoreau

One Path

My path on this earth is a spiritual one. For many years, I'd avoided this path, denying the very essence of who I am. Every moment of my life has reminded me of my path. As my moments of denial draw to a close, I find within me messages that I know I must voice. I know now why I walk this earth. I am a messenger. Even in those moments when I do not behave as one, I am a messenger. Even in those moments when I do not believe that I am one, I am a messenger.

I write this book not only because I choose to, but also because this is my purpose for being. My purpose is not unique. It is no different from the purpose of all other human beings because we are all messengers. The only difference is that some of us know that we are and some of us do not. Some of us live as if we are and some of us do not.

For years I lived in a world that did not recognize these matters of spiritual awareness that I now speak of. That world that I imagined myself to be in rarely recognized this unseen aspect of life. I ignored the invisible calling within me in order to fit into this world. Yet, now I sense this same world receding into our past as many more people begin to consciously perceive an invisible world. It is from perceiving this invisible world, that I am able to write these words. I have become aware of my path on this earth.

I recognize this as a path towards one-ness. It is a path that everyone is on. This book may serve as pathway to perceiving one-ness, but it cannot teach you anything that you do not already know. You experience one-ness by your own volition. It is experienced directly through you. No one can give it to you because you are already on it. You may be reminded of it, but only you can allow yourself to know this experience. Only you can give yourself what you most desire. This is power. This is *your* power.

We cannot hold a torch to light another's path without brightening our own.
—-Ben Sweetland

Power

I'd been so horrified with life because of what I thought and how I felt about it, but not because of what it actually was. Awareness of this has brought me to a new understanding of life.

This wisdom is already with you: you are more than body and mind on this earth. You are the energy of life that can be observed, experienced, and expressed through the use of the body and of the mind. You always have the power to live your dream.

The path to living your dreams is one that leads you right back to yourself because it is within the recognition of self. Every path in life leads you right back to yourself—plenty of times—enough times for you to remember this one thing: 'your life is your own creation.' Once you have remembered this, you will know your power and embrace life with a new awareness. You will know that your power is demonstrated through your ability to act in spite of your thought or your emotion—to act so as to fulfill the promise of your greatest dreams.

I am writing this book, especially for those of you who experience powerlessness. To have you know that with certainty, change is possible, if you choose it. You see, my power was always with me, even when it seemed to be taken from me. It is because I *believed* that I had lost it that I spent years of my life experiencing powerlessness. My message to you is that power can neither be lost nor taken from you. Therefore, if you believe that someone can take or has taken power from you, consider opening up to a new view.

In writing this book, I create a new reality for myself. In this moment I am being exactly what I am choosing to be, doing exactly what I am choosing to do, with complete awareness that I am living in power, because I dare to do what I had once been afraid to do. No longer am I afraid to live.

I now live in power. As a result, I am able to celebrate and appreciate my moments of powerlessness. I remember becoming so frustrated with life and crying out to our universe: "is this all there is?" Now I share with you–as a messenger of love, the answer that I received. These messages of love are already with you. They lie submerged within you. Awaken now, to this possibility.

Most powerful is he who has himself in his own power.

—-Seneca

The Possibility

When you allow yourself to experience life from a larger perspective, you open yourself to endless possibilities. This is because life is meant to be experienced so as not to limit your idea of you, but to enhance it. You can assume a different perspective about your life at any moment, but first you must choose to do so. To make this choice, know that you *have* a choice. You have a choice because at any given moment, there are endless possibilities for you to be a different you.

When you choose to see life from a larger perspective, for example, you begin to understand your self as bigger than and as grander than you once imagined your 'self' to be. You can know yourself as the beauty of a sunray, the freshness of the air, the blue of the sky, the dust of bodies passed, the pulsing energy of a love song, and the stillness of a tree. You can know yourself in un-imaginable ways. You can know yourself as the intangible 'no thing' aspect of life.

When you begin to see yourself from a larger perspective, your body takes on a different form. As you gaze unto the stars, trees, animals, and people that make up our universe, you will experience your new body. You will consider everyone and everything you see a part of this new body; a part of your own being.

In other words, you begin to experience your 'self' as a part of the one-ness of life. This experience will differ from your previous experience of life because you will know your self as part of a larger family. You will understand that to fight another is to harm your-loved one; that to pollute the earth is to pollute your own backyard; that to allow another's child to starve, is to allow your own child to starve; and that to believe yourself unworthy of love, is to reject the power that sustains you and all of life.

Perceiving the endless possibilities of life is an experience of living in a world of one-ness. You inhabit this world with a new body, a new heart, and a new mind. All of which, will be larger and grander than the body, heart, and mind you now experience as 'having.' The Universe will be your body and your heart will be within the rhythm of our life cycles. Your mind will be the essence of that which you perceive.

To perceive the possibility of one-ness means inhabiting a new world; a world made new through you—-through your willingness to "see" a new world. A world made new by believing in your own greatness. A world made new through the courage of letting go your old belief in powerlessness.

I invite you into this world. I invite you to invite others. Together we make it visible for them to inhabit. Together we can awaken our 'world-home-body' to experiences of unconditional love and unheard of experiences of compassion and harmony. I invite you to look into this new world. What is it that is new? What has changed?

Could it be possible that the world is transformed because you transform it? Is it possible that the manner in which you gaze unto the world renders it and *you* transformed? Could it be possible that how you "see" the world determines how gracefully you move in it? Is it possible that the transformation you seek is achieved in changing your inner perception of self?

Could it be that you've been experiencing a limited version of life and missing out on a grander knowing of it? Could it be that a world of peace resides within each and every single one of us...waiting to be freed? Could it be that the world is meant to be experienced as wondrous by all? Could it be that we have barely begun to explore just how glorious life is? Could it be that there is nowhere else for you to go to experience heaven? Could it be that everything you have ever desired is here now and ready for you to experience?

A Path to Living Your Dreams

What do you say? What do you say to the possibility of life lived in one-ness? Do you reject the possibility or do you embrace it? Do you shy away from it or do move toward it? Do you not yet perceive it speaking through you? In case you haven't already noticed, the decision to transform yourself and the world rests with you. This decision can only be made from within you—you, who are also a part of me. What will be your choice?

"You must be the change you wish to see in the world."
—-Mahatma Gandhi

Choices

Many people do not believe that they choose happiness. They believe that happiness is within the things that they will possess. They believe for instance, that when they have a nice home and a nice car, they will be happy. Some believe that a particular 'some-one' will 'make' them happy. Life times are spent with the stress of attempting to find ways to guarantee the presence of certain things and certain people in their lives.

I tell you, nothing can cause you to be happy, but you. Not a thing in the world can bring you joy, but you. Joy is within you! Happiness is in 'how' you behold the world and its manifestations. *You* determine the amount of happiness you experience.

Until you choose to be joyful in your present life, you will spend your life acquiring things only to experience them as a burden. The burden is created because nothing and nobody can be the source of your happiness, but you.

A Path to Living Your Dreams

Happiness is not within a car or a house, or another person, or even a million dollars, for that matter.

To live a burden-free life means becoming aware of this obvious, but often overlooked idea: 'the world is neither happiness nor sadness. It is neither cruel nor unjust.' The world is whatever you decide it to be. You determine your own experiences of the world through your thought and emotion about it. Nothing that you see and nothing that occurs has significance, except the significance you give it.

So, stop searching for happiness. Stop looking outside of you for joy because joy is within you! Joy is held within your *outlook* of life. It is in how you *look out* at the world. Do you look with sadness or do you look with joy? Do you look with optimism or do you look with pessimism? Do you look with wisdom or do you look with ignorance? Do you look with love or do you look with hatred? This is for you to choose. Your decision is the creation of your life experiences.

When you have to make a choice and don't make it, that in itself is a choice.

—-William James

Creation

Your life is made up of ideas, some from messages that span from the beginning of mankind, some that are passed on to you through others, and some are ideas that you create from your own intention. If you wish to transform your life, change the ideas you hold about your life. You experience your ideas simply by conceiving of them. You are always experiencing your ideas.

As children, we were not told that all the things we were taught to us were "made up." We were not told that all ideas of right and wrong, better and worse, were in actuality interpretations of the world passed unto us by those who had direct influence over our belief systems. Little did we know that we behaved in ways that were influenced by those we paid the most attention to, and that the combination of ideas we inherited from others, manifested the reality that we encountered.

The physical world is always subject to interpretation. How do you interpret your world? How do you interpret everything that is now occurring in the world? How do you interpret what others in your personal life do and say on a daily basis? How do you interpret what they do not say and what they do not do?

It is important to pay attention to your own words and your own actions because all that proceeds from you is also subject to interpretation. No thought of yours is unheeded. No spoken word of yours is unheard, even as you speak in silence. Although, it may seem that only those closest to you are affected by your words and deeds, know that your words impact the entire world. This is because there is only one being. There is only one life here on earth and you are a part of it.

Some of us did and do still attempt to change our lives by trying to change the physical conditions of our material world. Often we find our efforts to be futile. We find that when we try to change other people and the particular circumstances of our lives, we very rarely succeed in changing things and never in a lasting and meaningful way.

We do not realize that it is change in perception that produces our intended experiences. We do not realize that in order to change our experiences, we must change who and what we pay most attention to. We do not realize that to pay very close attention to what we desire is to acquire the belief that is necessary to experiencing it. Little do we recognize that the way to change the world is to change the way we perceive it because when we do this, we change the way we experience it.

The way to change your life experience of the world outside of you is not to change the world outside of you, but to change the world *inside* of you. This is true because the world is perfect as it is. Imperfection of the world exists only in how we perceive it or rather, how we judge it. It strikes me how poorly we think of ourselves. I wonder at the messages that we bring to one-another on a daily basis, fear-based ideas that are too often after being received, believed. There is no such thing as 'too short, or too tall, or too fat,' unless and until you compare it to something else. Yet, we are incomparable beings! Each and every single one of us is unique and different. Not a thing in the world is the same. This is why everything is perfect—-perfect by its own right and by its own design.

We fail to see our perfection because we are too wrapped up in comparing ourselves, and trying to transform our-selves and others, so that we can achieve a likeness that is not possible. This is the reason for insanity in our world. This is the basis of personal and world conflict. It is time now that we stop our insanity! You can play a huge role in this if you choose. Begin honoring yourself and others by accepting differences. Begin forgiving what and whom you perceive of as bad or wrong, by accepting the perfection of all things and all people. This is how to bring love into the world. Stop participating in the insanity by attempting to change the world through non-forgiveness and non-acceptance. Seek instead, to be more forgiving and more accepting of your self and others.

This is what we must continually remind our children. We must remind them the power of choice. We must remind them that they have the power to choose what to believe in and what not to believe in. We must remind them that through perception, they create their own experience of life. Do not wait that they should grow into adults who feel powerless in the face of their circumstance. Do not wait that they should believe that change is achieved through the means of forcing another to change. Do not wait that they should believe that they are always right and others are wrong, that their race is superior to another's, or that their religion is better. Do not wait that they should believe things about themselves that would destroy them and their world.

Ideas are at the root of creation.
—-Ernest Dimnet

Truth

As I write words flow through me, and I pause now and then, allowing myself to receive from spirit what I am meant to share with you and others on this earth. I know that I live a dream. This dream has yet to be seen by many others...yet even now as I write, I paint it for the world to see. It exists inside of me, in my mind's eye. A whole new world springs from within me, a beautiful world that floods my being with love. I know that this is why I live. I live to live this dream... this dream that I had been so afraid to believe in.

It matters not what word that follows, I had come to believe that to believe in my dreams was 'too flighty' or 'too unrealistic,' always 'too...something.' I had come to abandon the world of make-believe because I told myself that it was untrue. I felt out of control because I had lost sight of my power— my ability to decide for my-self what truth I wanted to live. I believed my own truth less than I believed another's. Life had become for me, a process of following rules, rules that made me nervous all the time for reasons I could not comprehend. Yet, now I understand.

To live your life is to experience your truth. Who determines your truth? Who decides what is true for you? All the truths I had been taught to believe in led me to this wisdom: that there is no truth. Truth is relative. It exists only for those who call upon it. Even then, it materializes in varying forms and different degrees to every individual. I know that all who live eventually come to this knowledge.

There is never any truth, except what you choose to believe. What you believe to be true is what you experience in life. You need not wait or look for truth because it is something that you *choose*. Every encounter you have in life presents you with this choice: to believe or not believe? You are never without this choice. In choosing, you use your power and call forth the reality of your truth.

There is no particular truth about anything in life because there are endless ways in which to interpret life. If truth is always changing, why live as if it is not? Why argue and harm each other over what is 'believed' to be true or not true? Is it not yet evident that truth is based on one's own choice of truth? Why deny yourself the choice of believing in your dreams?

Furthermore, why not now choose your own beliefs about your-self and your life? The next time someone calls you weak, or ugly, or stupid, not good enough, or un-realistic or whatever 'truth' they would have you believe, what will be your choice? Will you make the choice *not to* believe the ugly things you hear not only about yourself, but also of this world you live in and wake to on a daily basis? Will you choose to believe instead that you are Greatness? Is it not time now that you take control of your life and live it by deciding your own truth?

Every time a child says "I don't believe in fairies" there is a little fairy somewhere that falls down dead.
—-John Matthew Barrie

Why Wait?

I know now how dreams come true. Of course, I recognized the importance of having dreams: of painting a future with my mind's eye, the things I desired to accomplish in life. Intuitively, I have always known that I am a dreamer on this earth. Perhaps, this is the case for you, too?

Although, I'd spent many moments envisioning the life of my dreams, there was something very important that I was unclear about. What I did not realize and could not grasp before was that I could live the dream of my future, now. *This* is how dreams come true. Your dreams come true when you choose to live as if everything you've ever desired is already with you.

"But, what if it is not?" you ask.

To you, I say that there is nothing that you can conceive of that is not already with you. If you do not experience 'having' (what you conceive of in your mind), know that this is because you continue to behave as if you lack having it in your present reality. Dreams can only fail you if you fail to believe in them enough to live them.

I used to believe that the things I desired were in the future; that I would have to wait for them to become the truth of my reality. I waited for my desired future for many years. I waited until I got tired of the experience of waiting. Now I share this message with others: be willing not only to dream, but to live your dreams...now. See the future as now. Live the future now. The future *is* now. There is no other time for the future to play itself out, but right here and...now.

Why substitute your happiness for waiting? This is madness! Some of you may claim that you are not waiting. Yet, if you are one who says to yourself that you are 'stuck somewhere, or to a friend: "if only...such and such," then you are waiting. What do you wait for? For conditions to change? For others to change? For someone to come into your life and change things for you? Are you waiting for the 'right moment' to present itself to you?

I tell you: the right moment is always now. This is because there is no other moment. If you are not happy now, then you are waiting to be happy. If you are not now doing what you enjoy, then you are waiting for joy. What do you wait for? Courage? More love? More money? When will you ever experience these things if your time is taken up with waiting? When can the future of your dreams be played out in your life if you are unwilling to live it now, in *this* moment?

A Path to Living Your Dreams

In each moment you can practice not waiting by being as you have always desired to be. As you dress for work, or as you walk down a staircase, or as you drive to the grocery store, or as you walk into your home. Every living moment is a part of your dream coming true. How do you choose to experience your dream?

Don't wait for extraordinary circumstances to do good; try to use ordinary situations.
—-Jean Paul Richter

Manifestation

To live your dream, be aware of your ability to manifest. This ability is within all of us. The decisions that you make as to how you express yourself is what determines your physical manifestations. This is how powerful you are. If you are to master it, you must begin to practice this skill.

In this moment, I am practicing manifestation through my writing. Not only do I practice manifesting a book, I also practice manifesting my thoughts, emotions, and inner wisdom. Every day I write so that I can practice and sharpen this skill. I could just have easily chosen a different physical representation for self-expression. I could have decided for instance, to manifest greeting cards, or gray t-shirts, or videotapes, or key chains to express myself. I have chosen instead to write this book.

The art of manifestation is no more than the act of self-expression. If you wish to manifest what you desire, use your life as an expression of your desires. Some of you would deny your ability to manifest. I ask you: have you never written a poem, or drawn a picture, or built a sand castle, or taken a trip you always wanted to, or sung a song, or expressed an idea, or lost some weight, or gained some? Have you never taken a desire that is within you and turned it into something that everyone can touch, hear, smell, taste, feel, sense or know? Have you never made visible to others what would have remained invisible? I say to you that there is nothing that exists today that is not a manifestation.

Indeed, we exist in a world of endless manifestations. All of them are unique because they come from unique sources. If you do not understand this, you will feel as if you have little to contribute to the world. You will worry that what you desire to manifest will not be considered valuable. To you I say again: *everything that is manifested is unique*. This is true because every individual is unique. No one is exactly like another. When you express your-self, you in actuality, express your uniqueness. Only you can manifest for the world the gifts that are within you because *the value is within your uniqueness*. So, do not fear to express your uniqueness. Practice instead, and sharpen this skill. Do it now and manifest treasures for our world to behold.

You are unique, and if that is not fulfilled, then something has been lost.

—-Martha Graham

Unconditional Value

How much value do you perceive in yourself? How worthy do you believe your-self of a joyful life? Do you imagine that because you have anger within you, or that you feel afraid, or that because you have not experienced love as you have imagined it—-do you believe because of these circumstances, that you are unworthy of happiness? Do you suppose that because you sometimes experience feeling inferior to another that you are not worthy of a great life? Do you imagine that because there is no one else in the entire world like you, that you are not valuable to our world? Just in case no one has already told you, know that you are very valuable.

There is no part of life that is not valuable. This is the truth of life. Since you are a part of life, this is also the truth of you. You are that which is valuable. Your life is valuable. Your experiences are valuable. Everything about you is valuable. Just because you experience deep pain in you, does not make you in any way less valuable than another. Just because you own fewer possessions than others, does not make you less valuable than them. Just because some seem to dislike you, does not mean that you are unworthy of love and goodness.

I would like for you to consider the possibility of unconditional value. Consider that the value of life is without condition. Consider that for instance, no matter your 'transgression' or those that have committed by others, none of these things are a measure against the value of human life. Consider that every event and condition of life is a blessing and that everything you think is wrong is right. Consider that all things are right and perfect just as they are, even your anger, even your pain, even your sadness, and even your sense of aloneness.

What would you say if you were told that you have the ability to experience happiness, even in the midst of these things? Consider the fear, the war, the hunger, and suffering of our world. What if you were told that all of these aspects of life exist for your greater good? What if you perceived them as tools for expressing a new you and experiencing a new way of life?

To live in power is to know that all things have unconditional value. All situations in your life have a greater invisible purpose. The conditions that you call 'bad' exist so that you may use them to express and know goodness. They exist as valuable tools of creation. Do not be disheartened then, by your world of problems. Instead, take heart, because it is your greatest gift.

All things and all moments are gifts for you to use in defining your self in relationship to them. They exist that you may use them and experience your creative powers. There are no valueless moments in life. It may not be easy for you to 'see' what I am saying here, but you *will* know this truth when you choose to live your dreams.

I conceive that the great part of miseries of mankind is brought upon them by false estimates they have made of the value of things.

—-Benjamin Franklin

Freedom

When you live your dreams, you narrow your experience of life to the moment at hand, and experience freedom. Let us now speak of freedom. What is freedom anyway?

There are so many freedoms that we seek in life. Some of them are: time freedom, political freedom, economic freedom, and religious freedom. Many have dedicated their lives to achieving freedom. How will things be when you reach *your* freedom?

What do *you* seek to be free of? Is it your boss, your parents, your society that you seek to free of? What is freedom? Is it the absence of everything that you perceive of as bad in your life? Why do so many of us feel that we are not free? Is it really our economic, political, and social systems that cause our sense of captivity?

I daresay that the freedom we seek is even closer to us than we perceive. I have come to know that freedom is the state of being free of the thinking mind. It is the state where you are free from the stories you tell yourself about 'what happened or what could have happened', and 'what will happen or what should happen.'

Have you ever been "out of your mind?" To that moment where things not making sense no longer matters? To that place of total and complete acceptance of life as it is? That place of deep peace where time no longer exists and you encounter the perfection of life? Have you experienced that moment of 'no thought' where all there is, is now...that moment in between the past and future of your thoughts?

I know that all of us have been there because we are always there. Freedom is a state of being which we are always in. We are already free. The question is not if you are free, but if you are aware that you can experience freedom whenever and as often as you choose. Are you aware that you hold the key to your experience of freedom? The only thing keeping you from unlocking the gate is you...because you insist there is no aspect of you beyond the thinking mind and the physical body.

I used to feel trapped all the time. I felt it in the pounding of my heart whenever I experienced something that I did not want to accept in my life. My thinking mind would leap into the future and imagine the worst outcome. It would take me on journeys to painful moments in the past. My body would respond to the implications of my thoughts causing me to feel so uncomfortable in my body that I'd start to think that something was 'wrong with me.' I knew not the meaning of freedom. However, now I can share with you it's meaning.

Freedom is your total acceptance of the circumstances of your present life as they are. Freedom is in not allowing the jumping of your thoughts from past pain to future encounters with disaster—to be the story of what is now going on in your life.

No man is free who is not a master of himself.
—-Epictetus

Past

In order to transform your life, it is crucial to know that the past exists nowhere, but within your own thinking. Thinking of the past produces a play back of your past in the present moment. This playback can be very convincing. Many people can attest to this. They subject themselves to repetitiously re-living pain that they had experienced in the past. To them, life becomes a form of self-punishment. I know because I was one of these people.

I recently had this thought: if I were to move from my physical body in this very moment, would I be leaving knowing that my life was like I wanted it to be? I saw that I had yet to fulfill what I had envisioned for my life. I found that there were many things that I envisioned of accomplishing that seemed impossible to me. Why *impossible*?

Many of my greatest visions seemed impossible because I doubted my ability to make them so. I found that I had been basing my ability to create my future on my inability to do so in the past. In so doing, I had been using the past as a tool that limited me from living as an empowered being. After making this observation, I asked myself these questions: 'since the past no longer exists, what would happen if I repainted it? Would this make a liar out of me?'

The unusual thing is the answer I came up with. I became aware that repainting the past would not make me a liar at all, but a truth teller. I realized that if I did so, I would not only be telling the truth about who I am, but that I would also be living this truth. I realized that repainting the past makes it possible for us to tell the truth about life as we now see, experience, and know it. It makes it possible because there is no truth in life, but that which we say is true. Have you not read these words, already? Have you not been living out this exact message through your own life?

The past exists in you as thought. It is not a physical entity that can be experienced outside of you. To access the past, you must go inside yourself and observe your recorded thought about it. When you engage thought in this manner, you are in actuality, re-living memories. Although your memories may seem over-whelming, they are never more powerful than you are. You can release the hold of the past by acknowledging the power you have *now* in deciding your experience of the present moment. You can decide not to re-live your past.

You can decide to live your life by choosing not re-live it. It is how you spin the story of your past that makes your experience of life what it is now and what it will be. Therefore, your future is merely a newly spun version of the past. It represents your opportunity to create a new past and to live within a reality much like the past, but different, because you make it so.

What you are doing in life is learning to recognize your past for what it is. You are also learning to heal yourself by creating a new future. You have brought yourself to this moment in life to reclaim the power you have to live the life of your dreams.

Nothing changes more constantly than the past; for the past that influences our lives does not consist of what happened, but of what men believe happened.
—- Gerald W. Johnston

Illusion

The past exists, not so that you forget it, but so that you use it as a tool with which to create your present moment experiences. Pain and suffering from your past should not be forgotten, but be remembered in the present moment so as to enable the creation of happier moments. You experience freedom not only when you notice your power to release your past, but also when you recognize that you do not have to live in fear of the future.

The past and the future are *illusions*. Every living body carries its own unique version of the past and the future within it. This is also why truth does not exist. In life, a large number of people often decide to support a particular idea, and call it truth. What they call truth can more aptly be referred to as perspective.

The past and the future are illusions. They are not real. They exist in you and are experienced as realities when you live from within the belief that they are real. Re-living

One Path

the pain from your past is one such example. Experiencing anxiety in your present moment over what you imagine will occur in the future, is another example of living from within illusion.

You have the power to choose in every moment whether to surrender your past and let it be without you, or to be with you. There is no drug, no person, no thing outside of you that can free you, but you. The illusions of past and future are not to be ignored or forgotten. They are to be used for the purpose of deciding your present moment experience. They can serve as internal guidance systems when they are used as tools of creation. Too often, do we not use these tools. Or rather I should say, too often we *misuse* these tools. Too often do we attempt to change our future by re-living our past. Too often do we not envision magnificent futures for our world and ourselves. Too often do we experience life as a burden instead of as a gift.

The past and the future are your gift. To experience them as such, you must remember that they are illusions, which are to be used as tools for creating your intended purpose in life. From this perspective, they begin to serve you by reminding you of your own power.

Reality is merely an illusion, albeit a very persistent one.
—-Albert Einstein

Blindness

To spend your life feeling trapped is to experience a limited love. Observe your life and see what parts you are dissatisfied with because these are the parts that you must love. I can remember now just how dissatisfied I was with my life. Nothing I had was good enough. My hair was too unmanageable, my job paid me too little, my family was too dysfunctional, and the world was too violent.

I was rarely satisfied with my life because I judged it as not good enough. I didn't want what I had. I didn't want my life the way that it was. I could not bring myself to love my life because I was too busy finding fault with it. I could not consider my life as a part of the perfection that now I perceive. And so, I spent many moments of my life searching for a 'better life.'

Searching for a 'better' life meant feeling irritated and frustrated most of the time. It meant giving up the experience of inner peace and joy. It translated into choosing pain. There are many who live their lives in this manner. Millions of people are in a state of perpetual discontent. However, not all people are. I have been blessed in many moments to witness joy and peace within people living in the poorest conditions imaginable. I have been blessed to witness joy and peace within people who are so physically handicapped that you wonder how they manage to live. I have been fortunate to witness joy and peace within many of our children. I have seen complete joy and peace within people who live in constant physical discomfort and pain. These people have been my messengers. Their message is clear:

"Love your life," they say. "Love is who you are, so love who you are. Love is what you have, so love what you have. Love it all. There is nothing that cannot be loved. It is by loving who you are and through loving what you have that joy and peace are experienced. We have come to remind you of this and more...So, listen. Listen closely or you will miss our message. No one need live with out joy. It is in accepting your life that you find the satisfaction of being alive. To accept your life is not to resign yourself to the life that you now experience, but to love it. How else will you express and know love? What 'better' way is there to live your life, if not in love? Just as it may appear to you that we are imperfect, it may appear to you that your life is imperfect. Yet, all of life is perfection. See the perfection and rejoice. None of us is condemned. We are all a part of the same thing, this one being, which is love. So, go into our world and express who you are. Express the love that is within you. This is how you live in joy and peace. Remember always that love is limitless. Our lives are a testament of this truth. Live this truth. Live it now and bring more light into our world."

My darkness has been filled with the light of intelligence, and behold, the outer day-lit world was stumbling and groping in social blindness.

—-Helen Keller

The Light

Why are we here on earth?

We are here on earth to live.

Is this not what I've always been up to?

Yes and no.

I have lived and not known that I've been living. This is when I thought myself ignorant. I thought I didn't have the answers.

The answers to what questions?

I thought I didn't have the answers to questions like, 'what is the purpose for my life?'

The answer is so obvious I looked beyond it. I perceived life as a mystery.

The answer is so simple, my mind sought to complicate it.

Do you live in darkness?

For years, I lived in darkness. I scrambled in it, often closely watching others—-as if, they had the answers that I sought. Yet now I share with you some very good news. Even if you are now in darkness, you will one day perceive yourself as moving into the light. You will move into it *because* of the darkness. You will move into it because you will choose to.

Do you not see? It is *you* who determines *how* you live. Housed within you is everything you have ever needed to experience everything you have ever desired. The key to your dreams is in you. When you stop looking outside of you for the key and start looking inside yourself, then your heart will begin to warm. This will be the joy of your homecoming. When you acknowledge that you are what you desire, then you will know that you are the light. The key is made visible *through you* and *because of* you. This is why you are never without answers to *any* questions. This is why you need no longer stumble in darkness.

The light of awareness within you is a life revelation. If you want answers, know that you can have them in any given moment because they are already with you. They are within every aspect of life, awaiting your recognition. Every aspect of who you are answers what you think you do not already know. You are never without comprehension of life, because this understanding is within you.

The most incomprehensible thing about the universe is that it is comprehensible.

—-Albert Einstein

Space

It came so that I existed as an outsider to the world. No matter the situation I found myself in, I felt a sense of disconnection. This sense of disconnection prevailed over most of my experiences. It was as if I was a stranger looking in on the world. I was rarely plugged into any sense of comfort, love or self worth. The loneliness that I felt was painful, but it was the fear within me that was paralyzing.

I realize now that my sense of disconnection gave life to my fears. It is because I believed myself to be separate from others that I experienced very little comfort in being human. It is because I imagined my-self to be alone in the world that I felt alone. Now I know a different truth. This truth is in the path toward one-ness through which I now exist.

Look to the space that surrounds you. Space supports and makes possible our perception of materialism. Although very significant, we pay so little attention to this aspect of life. We often refer to space as "nothing." We are correct, because it is 'No Thing.' Space is not a particular thing, like a chair or a tree or a person. Space is what connects us to all things. It is the bridge between all of the things that we perceive as separate from us. All things are weaved unconditionally through space.

Space explains how it is possible that we are all *one*. It gives birth to all that exists. It is the constant in our world of change. It adapts to the changes of our material world, never disallowing us our creations. It holds us together. Were space to disappear, we would not be able to deny our one-ness. We would all mesh into a smaller body. A body the size of a thumbtack—-some would say.

Space would appear to keep us apart from one another and what we most desire. But does it really? Is it not just as conceivable that space keeps us together? Is it possible no matter how much space is between you and what you desire, that it is only because of *how* you perceive space, that you believe and experience alone-ness and separate-ness? What if you believed that the space between you and all things is what links you to those things? Do you suppose that your experience of life would be transformed? Would you continue to be worried and anxious about being separated from things and people?

The more space we put between us, the more we tend to perceive ourselves as being separate from one another.

One Path

However, when we to stop and pay attention to space, we bear witness of the one being of life of which we are a part. Space makes possible our perception of all the different aspects of the one being, which we call life. To accept or to justify the idea of separateness is to deny the connectedness of life, and to perceive alone-ness where there is none. Through space you can remember your one-ness with others and move into the most powerful state of being there is. It is the presence of your entire being. It is knowing one-ness.

Space is to place as eternity is to time.
$$\text{—-Joseph Joubert}$$

One-Ness

My words return to a message of one-ness. The more I speak of our one-ness, the more I experience it. What I speak of now becomes the reality of my experience. Such is the power of being human.

Where once I would not have been able to conceive of it as such, now I perceive my life as an instrument through which one-ness is remembered and experienced. Every time I sense unease in me, I know that I have lost my perception of one-ness. I know too, that alone-ness and hopeless-ness arise from forgotten one-ness. I no longer remain with unease for as long a period as I used to because I remember this wisdom.

This wisdom is awakening within the hearts and minds of humanity. Do *you* remember your one-ness with me? Do you remember your one-ness with every human being you come into contact with? Do you remember that we are all of the same substance? Do you remember that we are all made up of the same stuff? ...This stuff that we call life.

It is my intention that you remember, as I have come to remember, that nothing need prevent you from experiencing the life of your choosing. It is my intention that you are able to recognize your ability to choose your experience of life in every living moment. In order for this to happen, a new understanding of yourself *and* your world must be brought forth.

This new understanding proposes a new *role* for thought and emotion in your life. It suggests that you conceive of your thoughts and your emotions in a different manner. It does not propose that you abandon these tools. Rather, it asks that you embrace them. It does not ask you to forget who you think you are, but to remember who you are, at an elemental level. It asks that you remember that what makes-up life is all the same thing. When you remember this, you will know of one-ness.

The world we see that seems so insane is the result of a belief system that is not working. To perceive the world differently, we must be willing to change our belief system, let the past slip away, expand our sense of now, and dissolve the fear in our minds.

—-William James

Inner Perspective

When you experience one-ness, you "see more" of life than you already do. In order to do this, simply be willing to see more. Many people are not willing to. They would rather stick to their convictions, to their own ideas of good and bad, right and wrong. They would rather argue their point of view than experience another.

Seeing more of the world can be a frightening prospect. Some people do not want to experience anything beyond what they know because they fear what they might see. They fear that they might "see" something painful or something that they could not handle. For example, I feared being successful because I imagined that I would encounter experiences that I could not handle. My perspective on success changes the more I broaden my perception of it. Broadening one's perspective is what we call learning. We send our children off to school so that their perspectives might be broadened. This is the process of growing up which describes how we evolve as human beings.

The more we expose ourselves to new things and ideas, the more we know and experience of this world that we exist in. There are so many different ways to see the world. If you get nothing else from this book, just leave with this knowing: *There are endless ways in which to see the world.* Make sure then, to see the world in a way that pleases you because this will determine how you experience it.

To create a lasting transformation in your life is to enlarge your perspective. Enlarging perspective is often perceived as the exclusive act of examining more aspects of our physical world. Enlarging perspective as I speak of it, involves the world inside you. Everyone has an inner world. It is what makes people tick. The world inside you determines how you experience the physical world that you perceive outside of you. Your inner perspective allows you to see more than what is physical. It allows you to experience yourself as a being of one-ness.

If you look on to the world and all you see are dense objects spread out on the earth's landscape, know that your perspective is limited. If you look and see the objects and envision the life force within them, then your perspective has grown larger. If you see the objects, envision the life force within the objects, and feel the vibration of this energy within yourself as a part of you, know that your perspective has grown to encompass the interconnected-ness of all things. When your perspective grows to a level where you see how everything is connected; when your perspective grows to a level where you experience everything as a part of the same thing and as a part of you, then you will know one-ness.

In the perspective of every person lies a lens through which we may better understand ourselves.

—-Ellen J. Langer

Opportunity

Within each moment is an opportunity for re-birth. You can be a new you in every moment. You can experience a new you right now. Who you are now does not have to be based on who you were last year, or yesterday, or for that matter, the last second that just passed. Just because you are angry now does not mean that you have to be angry in the next moment. You can choose to be happy in spite of any anger. You do not have to go through life re-enacting the same experiences of who you are because you believe that have been permanently defined by them.

In each moment there is an opportunity for you to start over. In this moment, you can completely change your life. If you are unhappy with your life, use this opportunity to be happy with it. You do not have to keep re-acting the same way to the conditions that present themselves to you. Do not fret over moments of your life that have passed. Those moments exit so that you may use them as guidelines to creating new experiences. So, determine who you want to be and be it now in the midst of any life situation.

Enter every moment consciously by being what you choose. If your choice is to be happy, then be happy, no matter what! Even as your thoughts start to go all haywire and your mind tries to re-live a painful moment in your past, be happy *now*. Even as thoughts of worry cross your mind and as you begin to agitate over something that 'might' not occur the way you desire, be happy *now*. Even as your body is wracked in heartache, be happy *now*. Now is your only opportunity to be whatever you choose to be. Be happy because you have chosen to be so. Be happy because there is no better way to be.

Each moment is an opportunity to remind your-self that you have the power to decide your truth. Only *you* determine how to experience the present moment. This is your power. Acknowledge your power by using it. Use it to decide what your life will be about. Use your power and live as one who determines your own experiences.

Within every moment lies the opportunity for you to live in power and to experience your own Greatness. Accept the opportunity to know your Greatness. You can do so simply by choosing to be a person of Greatness. You can do so by embracing who you are and by *being* whoever you choose to be in every living moment.

One Path

Every moment is an opportunity for transformation. Do not miss the opportunity to transform your life by denying your ability to do so.

We are confronted with insurmountable opportunities.

—-Pogo

Action

Are you willing now, to consider the possibility that you are the creator of your life? That you have the power to choose at any point what your experiences will be? Are you willing to perceive yourself as capable of all of these things, and more?

The choice is yours to make. You have a choice in the role you wish to play on this earth. You always have a choice as to how you will participate in life. Take a good look at the word *action*. Actions are our acts of life put into motion. Through our acts, we create our experiences. We act as mothers, sons, fathers, daughters, sisters, co-workers, friends, lovers, teachers and the list goes on. We are always acting.

Somewhere along the way, we forgot that we were acting. What role do you choose to act out now? What type of acting do you wish to employ? Do you choose to act as if you are angry all the time or sad? Your actions *are* controllable.

One Path

Do you choose to act as if someone else is 'making' you act as if you are sad or mad? Look closely at your life and examine what roles you've picked out for yourself. Become aware of them so that you may choose a different way to act out your life whenever you wish. This is your power. You are that which controls your actions.

Do you not see now that you make up your life as you move along it? It could be said that you are a performing artist. Somewhere along the way, you chose your career; you chose the type of person you would be. Perhaps it was your father or your mother or someone who you've probably never even met, who inspired to be who you are today? Do you not see now that you act in ways that reflect your belief about your self and your world?

You act out your beliefs in every moment. Just as you are now making up your life so too, am I making this book up. Everything I am saying here is made up. I am inspired to the role that I am now choosing. You may choose at any moment to call anything that I write 'non-sense' or you may choose not to. It matters not what you choose. Just remember one thing: all of life is made up! So, believe whatever you choose. No one decides for you except you. And what you decide about your self and your world, you will demonstrate through your actions.

All of life is made up! So, stop behaving as if there is only one way for you to be. There are so many ways for you to be. All are for your choosing. If you choose the role of victim, you will feel like a victim and act like one. If you choose the role of creator, then you will feel creative and use every moment of your life to create the life you desire. When you determine your roles in life, make sure then to choose joyful ones. Choose who you will be in this life. Choose how you live this life. You will always have the power to choose. Begin now to act as if you do.

Action is the bridge between the physical world that you perceive outside of you and the inner world that exists within you. This is how important it is. It is the difference between believing your truth and living your truth.

Thought is the blossom; language the bud; action the fruit behind it.
—-Ralph Waldo Emerson

Emotion

I have some reservations writing about emotion because I have only just recently begun to use them consciously as a tool of creation. Although I do not consider myself the best source of information when it comes to this topic, I shall speak my truth. As with everything I have written thus far, I remind you that nothing I write is to be considered "the truth." I write to express the views and perceptions that lead me to self-empowerment. I write for the joy of expressing myself freely, in spite of emotions that would have at an earlier moment, prevented me from doing so. Therefore, please discard any words that you deem as unsupportive to your own development.

No one should have to not live out their dream because they have allowed their feelings to hold them back from doing so. I know a man who truly understands this. Even now as I write about him, I know that he is moving steadily towards his dreams, and doing so, in the presence of intense emotions.

Emotion itself is never a problem. It is because we hold on to our emotions, that we transform them into obstacles. They become obstacles when we trap them inside of us, instead of releasing them. Many of us do not know how to release our emotions, and so, we fail to experience them as a creative tool.

Releasing emotion requires facing it and putting the focus of your attention on it. This is contrary to finding something else with which to occupy your attention. It might not be what you are used to doing. You might be accustomed to eating, drinking, sleeping, watching television, or delving yourself into work when your emotions make themselves known to you.

Your emotions make themselves known to you because they are a part of inner arena. They exist to reveal your inner state of being. They are messengers that seek your reception. If you turn away from them, you fail to receive their message. You must learn to release this messenger that is called emotion because it will not leave you until you do so. The case is not that emotions do not want to leave us, but that many of us do not allow them to.

In order to release your emotions, be willing to observe them. Observe them as if you are watching an emotionally charged movie. As you watch them, know that you are their observer. This awareness does not mean that you no longer feel your emotions. You still feel them, but experience them from a point of view that allows you to remember that, in all moments, you have complete control over them.

Just as there endless ways in which to experience the world, there are endless ways in which to experience your emotions. As an observer, you know that you do not have to "be" your emotions. You understand for instance, that just because you feel sadness or anger, you do not have to "be" sad or "be" angry. As an observer of emotion, you can even choose to experience your emotions as *not you*. For example, you can watch your body tense up with anger, and have the experience that "this is how my body feels like when the emotion of anger enters into it."

If you are one who believes emotion to be a hindrance to achieving your highest potential, perhaps now is the time for a new belief? Perhaps it is time to discard the notion that emotion is something that you must ignore or hide or purge from your life? Perhaps if you stop treating your emotions as if they are obstacles, they might prove not to be? You might find that they have always been attempting to steer you closer towards your dreams. You may even begin to experience them as the most wonderful tool of self-creation.

By starving emotions we become humorless, rigid and stereotyped; by repressing them we become literal, reformatory and holier-than-thou; encouraged, they perfume life; discouraged, they poison it.

—-Joseph Collins

Life Energy

There had been in me a buildup of pain. It was pain rooted in my perceived sense of injustice and alone-ness. In me it resided for many years, rarely if ever, expressed. I was afraid to express it because I thought that in doing so, it would cause more pain. I was not even sure how to express it. However, I now find myself expressing it and in the manner of my choosing. It is through this book, it is through these words that you read that I express and experience it in a healing way. I share with you so that you may know that through pain, many great things can occur.

We all have pain. Most of us just don't know how to express it and experience it in a supportive way. Instead, we pretend that it is not there and live our lives attempting to avoid facing it. I was not very good at hiding my pain. Although obviously my constant companion, I still pretended to others that the pain was not there, to 'save' myself from experiencing it.

Too many of us suffer because we do not know how to constructively use our painful feelings. We attempt to run from them as I used to. Perhaps we run because we just do not understand what emotion is? Perhaps if we understood emotion, we would not even consider running.

Emotion is the energy of life flowing through you. It is the physical manifestation of the energy of your thoughts. This is evident because the world we live in is made up of energy. Everything is energy. It could be said that energy is the common denominator of life. What you think about the energy that enters your human form, determines the experience you have of that energy. Life energy becomes a painful experience when you label it as something negative.

This is true because life is an experience of the shaping and exchange of energy. The words that you speak and the thoughts that you entertain are examples of how energy is exchanged. *This is the power of your word.* Whatever name you give energy is what you will experience of it. You craft your experiences depending on how you receive life energy. This explains, for example, why some people find certain things funny when others do not or why some people find certain things discouraging while others do not.

Every moment of your life is for your deciding. Finding something humorous or discouraging is one type of decision. Your mind operates in such a way that if you do not consciously make decisions, it will do so for you. It will use whatever is stored in your memory bank to produce your next experience. The question therefore is not *if* you make these decisions, but *how* you make them. Are you conscious of your decisions or are you not?

Everything in your life is a tool for you to use in deciding how to live your life. Emotion is but one tool of creation. Sadness exists that you may experience joyfulness; fear exists that you may use it to experience freedom from fear. Your emotions can be used to bring you closer to the things you desire. Will you acknowledge and use this tool or will you continue to ignore and run from it? Would you rather allow your conditioned mind to craft your experiences or will you decide them for yourself? The answers to these questions will determine how you will live your life.

In a world where you do not perceive your-self as the creator of your experience, it will appear that your thoughts and emotions control you. You might even claim that they cause you to behave in a particular way. I invite you to see it in another way. I invite you to experience yourself as the *cause* of the experiences that flow into your life.

You can know that you cause every event in your life when you decide to live as a creator. You can know your-self as a creator by deciding that you have a right to happiness, in whatever shape, or form or manner you imagine it. When you decide to do this, you will experience life as a blessing and not as a judgment against you.

The real difference between men is energy. A strong will, a settled purpose, an invincible determination, can accomplish almost anything; and in this lies the distinction between great men and little men.

—-Thomas Fuller

Love

It used to bother me how uncertain the world seemed. There was never a set code for me to follow to "be normal," or to "be successful," or to "be liked" by others. I sought normalcy in everything I did, but never found it. I looked for ways to ensure that I would always be loved, not knowing that in doing so I denied myself the experience of love that I sought after.

Let us speak of love. What is love anyway? I have come to know that love is all that exists. *Love is who you are.* It is in every aspect of life and it is experienced in all moments. Life decisions are in *how* you choose to experience love.

Love is a decision. You need not look for it. It is already with you. Love can be experienced as joyful or angry or possessive or painful or in whatever other way you choose. How do you choose to experience the love that is your life?

It may not be easy to accept that you choose your experiences of love. You may come to believe, as I once did, that you are a 'victim' of love; that love always leaves you behind. For whatever reasons you come up with, you may come to see your-self as a person who is not loveable. You may come to believe that love is only a temporary phenomenon in your life.

Your life experiences may seem quite contrary to what I am saying here about love. I for one, would not have believed what I am saying now a number of years ago. Shifting my perception of love was a choice I made only when the truth of the love that I believed in became unbearable. I could not bear the belief that I was not loveable just the way I am. I could not bear the thought that I should have to live my life proving my worthiness or working my way to being loved. I could not bear the thought that I would have to do certain things to be loved.

My experiences surrounding love made me all the more ready to abandon my old beliefs about love. What I knew of love was the pain I felt about the disagreeable way in which the people I loved seemed to behave. I thought that their actions proved that I was not loveable. The actions of people I barely knew, I took as supporting evidence of my un-loveable-ness.

I finally got fed up with looking for love outside of me. I got tired of living with the experience of 'lacking love' and expecting others to 'give me' love. The pain of being who I had come to believe myself as became so unbearable, that

One Path

I knew I had to find a way to create a different experience of love. I saw that I had been experiencing love in a way that did not reflect the love that I dreamed of. The moment I decided that I would live differently is the moment that I became aware that I had a choice. In life, we always have choices. The most elemental of these is our choices about love.

Love is a choice. You may not be able to accurately predict the events in your life, but you may always choose the degree to which you will experience the love that is in you. You may not be able to keep a 'loved' one in your proximity as you would like to, but you may keep your experience of loving them. *Your capacity to love is unlimited*. You may always keep your experiences of love and you may always experience the love of your choosing.

What is the love of your choosing? Do you choose an angry and jealous love? Do you choose a love that is vengeful and spiteful? In other words, do you choose a love that brings you pain? There are endless ways to demonstrate love. What ways do you demonstrate the love that you dream of? Are you always waiting for it to come to you? Do you not experience it as always with you? Do you expect that you will have to fight for love, or look for love? *How do you dream of love?* These questions are for you to answer.

We are shaped and fashioned by what we love.

—-Johann Wolfgang Von Goethe

Fear

Since love is all there is, then what is fear? Fear has been said to be the absence of love or the opposite of love. I choose a different definition of fear. I have come to know fear as an aspect of love. It is an aspect of love that can lead to various experiences of love. Fear can lead to great things if it is allowed to. For instance, one cannot experience courage without the presence of fear.

Fear is another way of looking at love. It is what you feel of love when you no longer trust in its un-conditionality. It is what you feel of love when you think that you do not deserve a joyful love. So yes, fear can be very painful.

In life, you often meet those parts of you that you fear. I see now just how many different ways fear has entered into my life. My biggest fear was of 'being found out.' I have done all sorts of things to hide my internal wounds from others. I had the belief that allowing others to see my wounds would render me suddenly un-loveable.

One Path

I would not now be writing this book were I not ready to confront every single fear within me. I am able to face my fears now because I am willing to let go of every reason I had not to. I no longer deny my Greatness. My whole life has been in preparation for this moment. All of the pain that I have experienced because of fear has not been in vain.

As for you, my friend, do not take these words lightly because what I am saying here may apply to you, also. Your pain does not have to be in vain. There is no randomness and purposeless-ness in fear. You will experience this as true in the moment you decide to give up your own fears. The moment that you choose 'to be found out' is the moment when you will reclaim your power from fear. In that same instant you will reveal a love from within you that cannot be denied.

Throughout the writing of this book, I have put into practice the messages that I am now conveying to you. Most of what is written here has come through me in moments when I quieted my mind and allowed myself to let go my thoughts. Most of what I have written here has been in the presence of fear. I have the fear of being judged. I fear to dig deeper into my-self than I already have. I fear being rejected. So yes, fear is still with me.

The difference in my life now is that I am choosing my experiences of fear. I have chosen to trust in the greatness of the words that I am now sharing with you, *in spite of* fear.

A Path to Living Your Dreams

I have chosen to live my own truth, *in spite of* fear. In living this truth, I abandon the idea that fear should ever stop me from creating the life that I choose. This too will be your truth when you decide that fear is not an excuse for not to living in power. When you decide to live from within this perspective, you will have a different experience of fear in your life. You will find it leading you beyond anything that would keep you from experiencing your truth.

The man who fears suffering is already suffering from what he fears.

—-Michael De Montaigne

Peace

Human history reveals an ideology of struggle for "life." We have fought against each other for power throughout history to guarantee life on earth. It is time that we put an end to this delusion. There is only life. Our world is only ever alive. The evidence of this is everywhere we look, because everything is alive. Even what we refer to as "dead" is alive. How many more bodies do we have to lie down before we realize that we do not have to "preserve human life?" How long do we continue our scenes of mayhem before we perceive the senselessness of trying to end something that does not end? Life never ends. It only changes form.

The irony is that the more we act on the belief that human life needs to be protected, the better we get at dismembering the human body. Today we have weapons that can create wide-scale destruction of the human form. We not only threaten human life form, but other life forms because of our belief systems. To continue to hold the same beliefs is to invite the creation of more efficient ways to end our present life form.

Even though we do not really die, our present day reality moves us ever closer to the possibility of the permanent transformation of the human life form. I know that intuitively enough human beings understand this possibility. This is why we have not already ended human existence. We are at a turning point in human reality. Ahead of us lies a choice: 'to continue living in our present form or not to?' I watch as wars break out and escalate all over our world and wonder how many of us will see in this, that some of our beliefs are self-defeating and are now back-firing on us.

This book would not have been complete if I did not speak on peace because we exist in a world that is enveloped in war. The world of peace remains invisible in the majority's present day reality. It is up to us to make it visible.

We must decide as a people how we would like to demonstrate our humanity. How much do we value the human form? Within every moment that occurs, we will be deciding. Frankly, I am more than ready to abandon the persistent idea of creating peace by watching bullets rip people apart. I tire of seeing the human body being torn to pieces by other human bodies. None of this would make sense if we were all to take part and share in the knowledge of our one-ness. We would not even consider playing out the type of self-destruction that we demonstrate today.

I do not speak against war because it is not something that I condemn. It is through war that we are able to choose a more harmonious experience of our humanity. War as in all things, exists that we may call forth new experiences as a people. It exists so that we may examine it and declare a new future for humanity, if we choose.

Prevalence of war in our world provides us with tremendous opportunities for peace. What concerns me is that human beings have come largely to believe that war in itself *works* at resolving world conflict. The power of the human being remains unclaimed because we have not yet used war as a tool of creation. Instead, war continues to symbolize and sponsor within many of us, even more destruction. The dilemma is that too many of us now believe that a world of pain and suffering is all that exists. Of course, there are those who see the world with new eyes and different perspectives. For this I am grateful.

It is a change of perception that I call for in our world. When we are able to perceive each other as *one being* rather than as 'enemies' at war on earth, when we are able to see that there is no separation between one human being and another, then we will stop harming each other. The nature of war speaks to our belief in separation. What we call war is no more than a declaration of separation. This is the ideology that we were born in to. It is the ideology that the vast majority of us live by. We do not have to continue to live by this belief because we can make the choice to change it.

For those who truly want to end the pain and suffering of war, know that war can become a thing of our past if we now choose to put it behind us, and experience it as a part of our past. We will begin to make this choice when enough of us choose to view ourselves as unified and begin to live this truth. There are many on our planet who are conveying this message. The fact that you are now reading these words demonstrates that this message continues to be spread and to be heard. Take heed then, the power behind these words.

War will not end through more war. War will end through our evolution. Our evolution is centered in our consciousness. Our consciousness rests in our hands. Transforming your own perspective and belief in a world of separation brings the world moments closer to a higher consciousness of peace. The end to war rests in our hands because we create the reality in which we live. This is the message that I share with you. To understand this message is to live in power. It is up to you to decide.

We seek peace, knowing that peace is the climate of freedom.
—-Dwight D. Eisenhower

Decide

It is important that you remember who you are. You are a being of life that needs nothing. This statement could be true for you if you decide to live as if it were true. This is what life is about. Life is always about deciding who you are. You always decide who you are in this world. This is your power. You can decide to be anyway you wish to be at any moment of life. This is your power. Believe in your power.

What good is it for you to believe? The good is in itself because you are good in it-self. Many have been searching outside of themselves for the Greatness that resides within them. They know not that they already have what they seek. Perhaps, you have not yet experienced this knowing? Perhaps, you have not been aware that it is through opening your-self up to knowing your Greatness that you experience your Greatness? The words in this book can lead you to this knowing, but can never be the knowing. Only you can know.

And so, I say to you, *know* that you need nothing because this will lead to the experience of your having everything. How do you live as if you need nothing? See the perfection of our world. See too, that your life is perfection because to live as if it is imperfect, could mean living in a state of powerlessness and victim-hood. It could mean suffering because of what you perceive of as an unjust world. It could mean participating in an endless drama of 'not enough-ness.'

What then, would it be like if you lived as though the world were perfect? Imagine a world of perfection. Imagine that in this world, concepts such as good and bad, right and wrong, and better and worse, do not exist. In this world of perfection, there is nothing that you need because it is with you already. You bless every moment, every person and every occurrence. You 'love your neighbor as you love your-self.' You know peace and how to share it with others. Now, imagine that the world that I just described is the true nature of the world you live in now. Imagine that you exist in this perfect world.

The world of perfection that I speak of might seem very different from the world in which you perceive yourself as residing in now. Yet the only difference lies in belief. Perfection in the world is experienced when you realize that it matters not what is happening, but *how* you experience your life in the midst of every occurrence. It matters not to you what occurs in the world outside of you because you live from the world of perfection that you perceive from within you. When you change your beliefs and decide to believe in your Greatness, you step into a world of perfection.

Living in a world of perfection means accepting the guarantee of unconditional love. Every moment of your life would be received as an opportunity to be what you choose to be and to experience your-self as you choose. You would see every moment and every occurrence of your life as an opportunity for you to use your power to re-define your-self and your experience.

I think that somehow, we learn who we really are and then live with that decision.
$\qquad\qquad\qquad\qquad\qquad\qquad$ —-**Eleanor Roosevelt**

Abundance

Within all of the messages that I share in this book is a formula. This formula is the perception of one-ness to which my words point. The perception of one-ness is a pathway to transformation that invokes a type of journey that many have been unwilling to traverse. However, a growing number of us are willing.

The path of one-ness is an inward journey. It challenges the ideas that are at the foundation of the world that a majority of us perceive today. It is an idea from whose own foundation is the empowerment of the human being. To live this idea is to know courage. To live this idea is to know the impossible and the invisible. To live this idea is to know abundance and perfection.

Abundance is a way of seeing the world. The experience of abundance comes from within you. We live in an abundant world, but we do not always see this. I will now share with you how I envision abundance.

Abundance is knowing that you will always have everything you could ever need or ever want. It is knowing love as unconditional. Abundance is knowing that you are not just some purposeless being on this earth. It is knowing that every second, every minute, and every single moment of your life is meaningful and valuable. Abundance is knowing that you can share with others everything that you are and everything that you have, without ever having to fear that there won't be more. Abundance is the experience of knowing that there is always more of what you desire, and that nothing you desire runs out. It is knowing that there is always plenty more of what you choose. Abundance is an idea. It is an idea from whose foundation is the perception of a perfect world.

We live in a world of perfection, but we do not always see this. For a very long time, we have lived as if our world is imperfect. But is it really? You might argue that the world needs fixing. You might now live your life attempting to fix it. My question to you is: could it be that nothing needs fixing? Could it be that the way in which you 'see' the world is blurred?

We are quick to blame our world for the problems that we perceive in our lives, but to what end, I ask? With all the fixing that everyone is up to, one would imagine that by now there would be nothing left to fix. To be sure, we have become a society that is bent on fixing things. Always we are up to fixing something outside of us, but rarely do we consider looking within ourselves for different answers. We blame the noise for our headaches, we blame our bosses for our lack of money, we blame the other person for our unhappiness, we blame the person of another race for our anger...or the other driver, we blame our parents for our 'failures,' we blame the other country for our violence. When will we stop blaming the world outside of us for our own limited perceptions?

Is the notion of a perfect world still too inconceivable for you? Let us take a journey into this world...

I never think he is quite ready for another world who is altogether weary of this.

—-Hugh Hamilton

Perfection

In our world of perfection, you often encounter what others call coincidences. Yet, for you, there is no such as a coincidence. You know that everything that occurs in your life brings you closer to experiencing of your dreams. You experience nothing as random. No longer do you walk away from such moments, calling them insignificant and abandoning the opportunity to live in power.

In our world of perfection, everything that occurs happens for your benefit. The moments that you once unconsciously re-acted to, you now act in response to, with awareness and purpose. You whisper a thank you to your fearful thoughts as you proceed toward your goal. You are grateful for your weakest thoughts because they remind you of your power...your power of choice. No longer do you hold yourself victim to your own thoughts.

In our world of perfection, you feel the pounding of your heart and reawaken to the anger you once felt from believing that you are unworthy of love. You stop for a moment and breathe in your new truth of one-ness. You feel the vibration of the energy of 'anger' with-in you your body. You embrace this energy as it graces your presence. No longer, do you react to your emotions. Instead, you observe them, acknowledge them as they travel through you, and experience them for what they are: different aspects of love. You choose a conscious response to your emotions and determine your own experience of them. No longer do you hold yourself captive to your emotions.

In our world of perfection, you recognize yourself as the creator of your experiences. You know that every moment can be used as a tool of creation. As you observe chaos in the outside world, you focus on the world of peace that is within you. By directing the focus of your energy on your own intention, you decide your own path in life and experience your-self as living in peace. No longer are you dictated by conditions outside of you. No longer do you blame any-thing or body outside of you for the way in which you experience life.

In our world of perfection, there is no obstacle that you cannot handle. You approach every moment within a grander recognition of life. You journey the earth smiling inwardly, your eyes reflecting joy, the expression on your face and the posture of your body indicating a calmness born from inner wisdom. You know that you are always in a position to experiencing the parts of you that you choose to know.

In our world of perfection, there are no strangers or unfair moments. Every person you meet you recognize as a part of you. Every event that occurs you identify as a symptom of choices made from a part of your own being-ness. No longer do you feel isolated from others or disconnected from the rhythm of life.

In our world of perfection, you encounter roadblocks that would seem insurmountable to many other people, but not you. You know already that 'how' you experience these roadblocks is a choice only you can make. As others perceive defeat and walk away calling themselves failures, you choose to see triumph and call yourself a success. No longer do you view any event in your life as a problem, but as a blessing and a superb tool with which to express and experience your Greatness.

In our world of perfection, you predict your own future. You know that every-thing you imagine about the future is a prediction of it. You understand too, that how much you believe in an "imagined future," and how skillfully you use your tools creation, determines how much of this future is to be experienced in the reality of the present moment. No longer do you imagine your-self to be incapable of creating the life of your dreams. No longer do you perceive your-self as unable to live the life of your choosing.

In our world of perfection, there are many moments that seem not so perfect. These are the moments when you perceive a world of separation. There will be parts of you that resist against experiencing imperfection. You may experience pain during these moments and at times your suffering will be so great, that you will want only to escape it. However, you will reach deep into your inner-wisdom and remind your-self what you have momentarily forgotten. You will remember that you are experiencing the effects of an illusion. You will remember that the illusion exists not to cause you suffering, but to be the cause of great joy in your life and your world. No longer do you live from within the illusion of imperfection. For you, there is only perfection...

And so, you create your own happiness. You find that when you choose to be happy, you *are* happy, in spite of any circumstance and for as long as you choose to be. No longer do you seek to experience your life from outside of you, because you know that every-thing you desire is *within* you.

In our world of perfection, you notice that there is only life. You observe the transformation of life and celebrate a new beginning in every moment. No longer do you fear an end to life. For you, life has no end because you recognize that life can only shift itself to different patterns and forms.

One Path

No longer do you live in fear of life.

Happiness resides not in possessions and not in gold, the feeling of happiness dwells in the soul.
$\qquad\qquad\qquad\qquad\qquad\qquad$ —-Democritus

Shape Shifting

We are shape-shifters, you and I. Life is always in a process of shape shifting. To live as though nothing changes or that nothing should change is a form of denial that causes only more pain in our world. If you do not remember now, while in your body, that nothing dies, then you shall remember when you shift from your body. Why wait though?

Why not now observe the evidence of this, while still in your body? Watch the rhythmic cycle of life, as the seasons shift. Watch as your own body shifts. Just as you did not die when you shifted from your non-physical form to physical form, so too, do you live when you shift from physicality to non-physicality.

Is it not conceivable that life is a process of shifting that does not end? Everyday we witness life shifting from the invisible to the visible, from the intangible to the tangible. Is this not how this book is now being created? Is this not how the reverse of the process of ice turning into water and then into condensation, is possible? Is this not the very nature of life evidencing itself to us? What more evidence do we look for that there is no death in life?

What more evidence do *you* need in order to stop ignoring the messages within your own being? Is it more pain that you call for in your life? How many more moments will you ignore the aches and pains within your own human form before you recognize that it is *you* who are calling yourself? Your non-physical self calls for your attention through your physical form. When you receive its call, you will experience the transformation that you have sought. This message is communicated to you in every moment of life.

Look to this message within your-self. Do not allow your-self to be distracted by what is outside of you because truth is within you. So, pay attention to your self. Do not resist against your internal messages because doing so is to manifest more of what you resist. So, welcome the messages that are within you and stop ignoring your own pain because when you do so, you carry it with you and contribute it to our world.

Moreover, stop treating what you think is negative as some sort of mistake. There are no mistakes! In life, there are no mistakes. Therefore, your pain has a purpose. To know this purpose, determine it by facing your pain and by allowing your-self to *feel it*. Feel it to its depth and uncover what is rooted there. This is how I have come to know my purpose. I now observe the suffering of people all around the world with a different understanding. I view my own suffering as a reflection of our world's suffering. Within this recognition, lies a choice. I am making the choice no longer to suffer.

Having made that choice, I enable myself to help others in our world. I did not know how to do this before because I believed that my own pain stood in the way. I did not know that I was the only one creating the pain, because I harbored within me hand-me-down beliefs, which diminished my ability to live in power. Now, I find myself challenging and re-placing my old beliefs with new ones. Some of these new beliefs I have shared with you in this book.

These truths are not meant to dissuade you from, but to lead you to your own truth. Do not accept anything that I have written here, rather, test it in your own life. Decide for yourself what messages you will use and discard those that do not work for you. My main message to you is for you to *live your own truth*. Live your truth by expressing it in whatever manner that brings you joy. This is how you bring more joy into our world. Always live your own truths. Not mine, not another's, but your own.

Nothing is impossible; there are ways that lead to everything and if we had sufficient will we should always have sufficient means. It is often merely for an excuse that we say things are impossible.
—-Francois De La Rouchefoucauld

Saying Goodbye

A few last words before I have this book published. Writing it has been for me, an enlightening experience. I hope that you have had a good look inside. However, if it appears to you that these words have come to you by chance, then look again. If you have the belief that you have not brought these words to yourself and that you have come to this book by accident, then think again. There is always another way in which to experience this moment. What will be your choice?

I choose now to continue on my path as an author and messenger. I choose now to say some goodbyes. Saying goodbye is yet another tool of creation. It is the tool that I am now using to experience moving this book along our path.

Goodbye to doing things that do not help people in the way that I feel most joyful with. Goodbye to living every moment as if I'm not *now* in it. Goodbye to waiting to write this book and publishing it in 'the future.' Goodbye to thinking that I am not deserving of happiness and wealth. Goodbye to being afraid to love those who have chosen their own path. Goodbye to believing that I am just a body and mind on this earth. Goodbye to believing that I am alone in our world. Goodbye to living as if am not a part of this one-being that is life...

I invite you now to say your own goodbyes.

The only thing I was fit for was to be a writer, and this notion rested solely on my suspicion that I would never be fit for real work, and that writing didn't require any.

—-Russell Baker

Note to the Reader

One Path is currently working on her second book and would love to hear your comments about this book.

She will soon be releasing audiotapes and CD's of her first interview as an author.

To contact the author with comments or to request more information about ordering the recorded interview with One Path, please email: one-path@myway.com

You can order copies of this book at: www.authorhouse.com, Online Bookstore.

Please invite your family and friends to order their own copy. Thank you for your support.

About the Author

Dynamic and entertaining, the author has a talent for communicating powerful messages. Born in Tanzania, East Africa, she is now a resident of N.J. She has a B.A. in Economics and Spanish from Rutgers University. Her passion is to live the life of her dreams and to inspire others to do the same.

Printed in the United States
24056LVS00002B/145